Practical Sermon Outlines

Practical Sermon Outlines

Russell E. Spray

PULPIT LIBRARY

BAKER BOOK HOUSE Grand Rapids, Michigan 49506

Copyright 1984 by
Baker Book House Company
ISBN: 0-8010-8240-4

PHOTOLITHOPRINTED BY CUSHING - MALLOY, INC.
ANN ARBOR, MICHIGAN, UNITED STATES OF AMERICA

Contents

1. Christ Relates to His People 8
2. Ever-Ready Prayers 10
3. Facets of Divine Love 12
4. Follow His S-T-E-P-S 14
5. How to R-E-N-E-W Your Faith 16
6. Let Go—Let God 18
7. The Winning Side 20
8. The Power of God Through Faith 22
9. Practice Makes Perfect 24
10. P-R-A-I-S-E the Lord 26
11. T-E-A-C-H Me, Lord 28
12. The Good Shepherd and His Sheep 30
13. Christian Duties in the World 32
14. God Brings Deliverance 34
15. God's W-O-R-D Teaches 36
16. How to Overcome Temptation 38
17. Miracle of Healing 40
18. Slow Down and Live 42
19. Spirit-Filled Christians 44
20. The Apple of God's Eye 46
21. The Dimensions of Love 48
22. The Essentials of Life 50
23. The Greatest Love 52
24. The Holy Spirit in Believers 54
25. The Jesus W-A-Y 56
26. The Value of Faith 58
27. What's Your Problem? 60
28. The Dynamics of L-O-V-E 62
29. Are You for Real? 64
30. Attaining to Spiritual Heights 66

31.	Coping with the "Daily Grind"	68
32.	Effective Workers for Christ	70
33.	Get with It for Christ	72
34.	H-A-P-P-Y Christians Are...	74
35.	How to H-E-A-R the Word	76
36.	How to Use God's Word Effectively	78
37.	How to Win Over Depression	80
38.	Jesus Christ, the Rock	82
39.	Reasons to be Cheerful	84
40.	R-E-S-T in the Lord	86
41.	The Christian's Stand	88
42.	Today's Instant Society	90
43.	You Don't Have to F-A-I-L	92
44.	Why We Should Keep F-A-I-T-H	94

Foreword

Practical Sermon Outlines deal with the difficulties of everyday living. They exalt the One who can solve all problems. "For the bread of God is he which cometh down from heaven, and giveth life unto the world" (John 6:33).

It is my hope and prayer that all who use and hear these outlines may seek to glorify the Christ who came "down to earth."

Russell E. Spray

1

Christ Relates to His People

"I am crucified with Christ: nevertheless I live; yet not I, but Christ liveth in me: and the life which I now live in the flesh I live by the faith of the Son of God, who loved me, and gave himself for me" (Gal. 2:20).

I. Christ Lives in His People
"I in them, and thou in me, that they may be made perfect in one" (John 17:23).
   A. Christ's presence brings comfort and reassurance. Even in today's troubled world we can be sure of His continued presence (Heb. 13:5).
   B. Christians are in Christ—"old things are passed away . . . all things are become new" (2 Cor. 5:17). Our desire is to please and glorify the Lord.

II. Christ Listens to His People
". . . his ears are open unto their prayers . . ." (1 Peter 3:12).
   A. It is sometimes difficult to be heard. Our voices are often drowned out in the noise and confusion of our busy times.
   B. There is always a listening ear in Christ. He hears our faintest cry. He gives guidance and direction to those who heed His counsel (Isa. 30:21).

III. Christ Looks After His People
"For the eyes of the Lord are over the righteous . . ." (1 Peter 3:12).
   A. Ours is a danger-filled society. Violence and crime have invaded countless homes, cities, and nations.

B. Christ is the Christian's source of protection. He watches over us, guarding and guiding our footsteps. We must trust and rely on Him daily (Ps. 56:3).

IV. Christ Labors with His People
"We then, as workers together with him . . ." (2 Cor. 6:1).
- A. Many Christians suffer feelings of rejection and aloneness when doing God's work. They need not, for God has promised, "I am with thee . . . I will strengthen thee; yea, I will help thee . . ." (Isa. 41:10).
- B. Christ helps us as we help the needy. He comforts us as we comfort the lonely. He shares His love with us as we share it with the unsaved.

V. Christ Loves Through His People
". . . love one another, as I have loved you" (John 15:12).
- A. The greatest need of our day is not for more possessions, pleasure, or power, but for the love of Christ.
- B. Christ loves through His people. Walls of hatred, greed, and resentment crumble when Christ's love is lifted up. "For charity [love] shall cover the multitude of sins" (1 Peter 4:8).

2

Ever-Ready Prayers

"Rejoicing in hope; patient in tribulation; continuing instant in prayer" (Rom. 12:12).

Most Christians need to pray more. The following points should help clarify the "when," "where," "what," and "who" of prayer.

I. Everyday Prayers
"Pray without ceasing" (1 Thess. 5:17).
   A. Many Christians are caught up in the rush of our busy times. They forget, or simply neglect, to pray as they should.
   B. We must discipline ourselves to pray and keep in a spirit of prayer throughout the day.
   C. To be effective, prayers of petition should be accompanied by praise (Phil. 4:6). The Lord is worthy of all our praise. We can never praise Him enough (Ps. 145:2–3).

II. Everywhere Prayers
"I will . . . that men pray everywhere . . . without wrath and doubting" (1 Tim. 2:8).
   A. Some feel that they can pray effectively only in church. Their prayer life is limited.
   B. Christ died on the cross to bring the human race back into fellowship with God. He is omnipresent (everywhere).
   C. We should talk to God wherever we are—at home, at school, at work, at play. Praying increases our joy and confidence (John 4:20–24).

III. Everything Prayers

". . . in everything by prayer . . . let your requests be made known unto God" (Phil. 4:6).

A. Christians often fail to pray about the little things in life. They forget that "the little foxes . . . spoil the vines" (Song of Sol. 2:15).
B. We must take everything to God in prayer—small or great, good or bad. We must surrender all to God's will. "And the peace of God . . . shall keep your hearts and minds . . ." (Phil. 4:6–7).

IV. Everybody Prayers

". . . pray one for another . . ." (James 5:16).

A. Some Christians fail to pray for others, especially those for whom they hold resentment or dislike. If indeed they do pray, it is "at them" rather than "for them."
B. God doesn't answer "snobbish" or "get even" prayers. We cannot truly pray for others and hold resentments against them at the same time (Matt. 5:44).
C. We must be filled with God's love to be enabled to pray for the wealthy and wanting, healthy and hurting, saint and sinner—everybody (1 John 4:11).

3

Facets of Divine Love

"But the fruit of the Spirit is love, joy, peace, longsuffering, gentleness, goodness, faith, meekness, temperance: against such there is no law" (Gal. 5:22–23).

Love, the first fruit of the Spirit, filters throughout all the remaining fruits of the Spirit.

I. Joy Is Love's Cheerfulness
   A. Many Christians are negative. Their lack of love causes them to view life with a depressive outlook.
   B. Christians who are filled with God's love are alive with cheer and joy. The joy of the Lord is attractive and influences others to come to Christ (Phil. 4:4).

II. Peace Is Love's Calmness
   A. Our world is desperately searching for peace. But there is little peace because there is little love.
   B. Love harmonizes the Christian's will with God's will, relieving tension, removing friction, and restoring calmness. "The peace of God . . . shall keep your hearts and minds . . ." (Phil. 4:7).

III. Longsuffering Is Love's Continuity
   A. Many project a poor Christian image because they are impatient. Love doesn't strike back with vengeance but overcomes evil with good.
   B. We must follow Christ's example. "Charity [love] suffereth long, and is kind . . ." (1 Cor. 13:4).

IV. Gentleness Is Love's Courtesy
   A. Millions in today's world are possessed with selfish and sinful motives. They are inconsiderate of the rights and feelings of others.

B. We must be mindful of others, extending the hand of love. "... be courteous" (1 Peter 3:8).

V. Goodness Is Love's Contribution
A. The goodness of love contributes to the rich and poor, educated and uneducated, high and low alike. It reaches in every direction to all people.
B. Love's goodness seeks to help those who appear to want no help as well as those who come for assistance (Acts 10:34).

VI. Faith Is Love's Confidence
A. Today's world is filled with doubt, fear, suspicion, and confusion.
B. Love's confidence leads to salvation, serenity, and security. This confidence is for those who come to God in simple, trusting faith (Heb. 11:6).

VII. Meekness Is Love's Compliance
A. "Humble yourselves ... under the mighty hand of God, that he may exalt you in due time" (1 Peter 5:6).
B. Love with meekness enables Christians to cooperate with God and others in the advancement of God's kingdom here on earth.

VIII. Temperance Is Love's Controllability
A. The love-filled life is a disciplined and balanced life. It gives God first place.
B. We would do well to follow Paul's example: "But I keep under my body, and bring it into subjection: lest that ... I myself should be a castaway" (1 Cor. 9:27).

4

Follow His S-T-E-P-S

"For even hereunto were ye called: because Christ also suffered for us, leaving us an example, that ye should follow his steps" (1 Peter 2:21).

The following points should encourage Christians as they strive to follow Christ's S-T-E-P-S.

I. S-peak Like Christ

"But speaking the truth in love, may grow up into him in all things . . ." (Eph. 4:15).

A. Christians may harm the cause of Christ and hurt their own influence by speaking harshly and unlovingly.
B. Christ spoke the right words at the right time and place—uplifting, healing, and helpful words.
C. To follow His steps we must speak with love, kindness, and understanding (Eph. 4:32).

II. T-hink Like Christ

"Let this mind be in you, which was also in Christ Jesus" (Phil. 2:5).

A. Many Christians lack victory because they allow negative thoughts to control their lives.
B. We must discipline our thoughts by replacing the negative with the positive. ". . . whatsoever things are of good report . . . think on these things" (Phil. 4:8).
C. To follow His steps we must habitually think pure, positive, and purposeful thoughts.

III. E-ndure Like Christ

"Consider him that endured such contradiction of sinners against himself, lest ye be wearied and faint in your minds" (Heb. 12:3).

A. When adversity strikes, some are ready to question or blame God. Others are tempted to throw up their hands in despair.

B. Christ endured the cross that was set before Him—with joy (Heb. 12:2).
  C. We must consider the way Christ endured and follow His steps, being aware "that in all things God works for the good of those who love him . . ." (Rom. 8:28, NIV).

IV. **P-ray Like Christ**
Nevertheless not as I will, but as thou wilt" (Matt. 26:39).
  A. Christians often tell God what they want rather than ask what He wants for them.
  B. In Christ's most crucial hour, a time when His very life was at stake, He prayed for His Father's will to be done.
  C. If we are to follow His steps, we must surrender totally to God's will and pray as Jesus did, ". . . thy will be done" (Matt. 26:42).

V. **S-erve Like Christ**
". . . and took upon him the form of a servant . . ." (Phil. 2:7).
  A. Christ preached to the poor, healed the brokenhearted, delivered captives, opened blinded eyes "to set at liberty them that are bruised" (Luke 4:18).
  B. To follow His steps we must help the less fortunate, comfort the lonely, and share Christ with the lost.
  C. Speak like Christ; think like Christ; endure like Christ; pray like Christ; serve like Christ. If we do these things, some day we will become like Christ (1 John 3:2).

5

How to R-E-N-E-W Your Faith

"And be renewed in the spirit of your mind" (Eph. 4:23).

The following points will assist in upgrading and expanding our faith. We need to R-E-N-E-W our faith.

I. R-eview Your Faith
"Examine yourselves, whether ye be in the faith; prove your own selves..." (2 Cor. 13:5).
   A. Check the quantity of your faith. How much do you have? Do you want more?
   B. Check the quality of your faith. Will it stand when the storms of life are raging? Will it prove true when the pressure is on? (Luke 22:31–32).

II. E-xpress Your Faith
"For with the heart man believeth... and with the mouth confession is made..." (Rom. 10:10).
   A. It is difficult for some shy people who have a retiring nature to reveal their faith. However, expressing one's faith helps to strengthen and expand one's faith.
   B. Faith is contagious. It spreads to bless others and glorify Christ. Jesus said, "... whosoever shall be ashamed of me ... of him shall the Son of man be ashamed ..." (Luke 9:26).

III. N-urture Your Faith
"... your faith groweth exceedingly..." (2 Thess. 1:3).
   A. Faith stops growing when it is neglected. Neglecting prayer, God's Word, church attendance, and involvement in God's work destroys faith.

B. Trials and troubles test the caliber of one's faith. But when one's faith is properly nurtured, trials may serve to speed its growth.

IV. E-njoy Your Faith
"... *for your furtherance and joy of faith*" *(Phil. 1:25).*
A. Sometimes Christians endure their faith rather than enjoy it. They receive limited benefits when they do.
B. You should enjoy the blessing and miracles that faith affords. The more you praise the Lord for His blessings, the more blessings He will send. (Ps. 107:8–9).

V. W-ork Your Faith
"Even so faith, if it hath not works, is dead, being alone" (James 2:17).
A. Work your faith and it will work for you. Be ready to lend a helping hand, comfort the discouraged, or share Christ with another.
B. Remember, nothing is too difficult for faith and God to handle—mountains, valleys, deserts, oceans. With God no adversary is too great (Mark 9:23). Renew your faith today.

6

Let Go—Let God

"And he said to them all, If any man will come after me, let him deny himself, and take up his cross daily, and follow me" (Luke 9:23).

If we would follow the Lord and be fruitful for Him, we must deny ourselves.

I. Selfish Measures
". . . in the last days . . . men shall be lovers of their own selves . . ." (2 Tim. 3:1–2).
- A. Millions in today's world are selfishly motivated. Their attitude is "Me first, me next, and me last."
- B. Many Christians are self-centered. Their outreach for God and others is limited.
- C. God's Holy Spirit is waiting to cleanse and empower for service those Christians who make a total commitment to Him (Rom. 12:1).
- D. Selfishness must go. When resentment, worry, and strife are completely yielded to God, He fills us with His love.

II. Sensual Pleasures
". . . lovers of pleasures more than lovers of God" (2 Tim. 3:4).
- A. Ours is a pleasure-seeking, pleasure-loving society. Many are hoping pleasure will drown their troubles.
- B. Instead of facing up to their inner problems, some attempt to cover them up with pleasure.

C. We must surrender our burdens to God unreservedly. He is able to carry them for us (1 Peter 5:7).
D. Sinful pleasures must go. When they do, God will replace them with His pure and wholesome joy (Ps. 51:12).

III. Secular Treasures
"For the love of money is the root of all evil..." (1 Tim. 6:10).
A. The love of money has destroyed the lives and souls of countless people. It isn't wrong to have money, but to love money is sin.
B. Many forfeit honor, home, family, and soul for possessions. They fail to realize that "a man's life consisteth not in the abundance of things which he possesseth" (Luke 12:15).
C. God must have first place in our lives. We must strive to lay up treasures in heaven rather than here on earth (Matt. 6:19–21).
D. The love of secular treasures must go. Earthly treasures rust and decay. Heavenly treasures are eternal.

7

The Winning Side

"We are troubled on every side, yet not distressed; we are perplexed, but not in despair; persecuted, but not forsaken; cast down, but not destroyed" (2 Cor. 4:8–9).

Although Christians are tempted, tested, and tried, they need not be defeated. They are on the winning side.

I. Troubled—but Not Distressed
"We are troubled on every side, yet not distressed..." (2 Cor. 4:8).
  A. Trouble began for the human race when man disobeyed God in the Garden of Eden.
  B. Christians have troubles but they have One to whom they can go and on whom they can depend.
  C. We need not be distressed. God will replace our worry and strain with His peace and rest (Ps. 37:39–40).

II. Perplexed—but Not in Despair
"... we are perplexed, but not in despair" (2 Cor. 4:8).
  A. There are many problems to deal with in our world. Millions of people are frustrated, confused, and perplexed.
  B. Christians are perplexed at times, but they are not in despair.
  C. While multitudes are losing hope and giving up in despair, our hope is in God (Ps. 42:5, 11). He never fails. The best is yet to come.

III. Persecuted—but Not Deserted
"Persecuted, but not forsaken..." (2 Cor. 4:9).
- A. Persecution has been the lot of Christians throughout the centuries. "Yea, and all that will live godly in Christ Jesus shall receive persecution" (2 Tim. 3:12).
- B. Persecution may come in the form of abusive treatment, in silence, or more subtle ways.
- C. We must trust in the Lord and rely on His promises. "I will never leave thee, nor forsake thee" (Heb. 13:5). We are on the winning side.

IV. Cast Down—but Not Destroyed
"... cast down, but not destroyed" (2 Cor. 4:9).
- A. Peter could relate to Christ's suffering because he, too, suffered (and died) for his faith. He also shared the life that Jesus gives (2 Cor. 4:10–11).
- B. We must be willing to suffer "for Jesus' sake." "If we suffer, we shall also reign with him..." (2 Tim. 2:12).
- C. Christians may be cast down at times but they need not be destroyed. Faithfulness to God brings victory both now and eternally (Rev. 2:10).

8

The Power of God Through Faith

"Who are kept by the power of God through faith unto salvation ready to be revealed in the last time" (1 Peter 1:5).

The following blessings are ours "by the power of God through faith."

I. Confidence to the Fearful
". . . be not afraid, only believe" (Mark 5:36).
- A. Today's world is a place of danger, violence, and fear. Many Christians lack confidence in God.
- B. Praying, reading God's Word, and loving God and others increases our faith. The more faith we have, the less fear we possess.
- C. The power of God through faith is the antidote for fear. ". . . The Lord is the strength of my life; of whom shall I be afraid?" (Ps. 27:1).

II. Calmness to the Fretful
". . . Why are ye fearful, O ye of little faith? Then he . . . rebuked the winds and the sea; and there was a great calm" (Matt. 8:26).
- A. The disciples were fretful. Their situation was perilous. Jesus rebuked their lack of faith and calmed the storm.
- B. Christians today often fret about circumstances over which they have no control. Like the disciples, they are of little faith.
- C. We must claim the power of God through faith. God is still able to calm the storms. He never changes (Mal. 3:6).

III. Composure to the Frustrated
"Let not your heart be troubled: ye believe in God, believe also in me" (John 14:1).
- A. In today's society millions live in frustration and perplexity. Sometimes Christians are frustrated, too.

B. Composure awaits Christians who cast all their care upon the Lord (1 Peter 5:7).
C. When we trust the Lord, resist evil, and remain steadfast in the faith, we become established, strengthened, and settled (1 Peter 5:9–10).

IV. Crowns to the Faithful

"... *I have kept the faith: Henceforth there is laid up for me a crown of righteousness...*" *(2 Tim. 4:7–8).*

A. Paul had been abused, shipwrecked, and left for dead, yet he kept the faith.
B. We must keep the faith also. A crown of righteousness awaits those who faithfully perform the tasks that God has given them to do.
C. We must be faithful in spite of the odds against us and regardless of how small our tasks may be (Rev. 2:10). God's power plus our faith not only brings confidence, calmness, and composure in this life, but a crown awaits the faithful in the life to come.

9

Practice Makes Perfect

"If ye know these things, happy are ye if ye do them" (John 13:17).

By practicing the following precepts, we can enjoy a happy and productive life.

I. Practice the Presence of Christ
". . . and, lo, I am with you alway, even unto the end of the world" (Matt. 28:20).
- A. Many Christians lack an awareness of Christ's personal presence. They are too busy with their own pursuits.
- B. We must take time to fellowship with Christ. Daily, hourly, and moment by moment we should maintain an awareness of His presence.
- C. Prayer, God's promises, and perseverance are needed to effectively practice the presence of Christ (Heb. 13:5).

II. Practice the Purity of Christ
"And every man that hath this hope in him purifieth himself, even as he is pure" (1 John 3:3).
- A. When Christ was here on earth, He set the example of purity for us to follow.
- B. Today non-Christian influences often cause Christians to let down their standards of Christian purity.
- C. We must practice thinking, seeing, hearing, saying, and doing those things that are consistent with the teachings of Christ (1 John 2:5–6).

III. Practice the Peace of Christ
Peace I leave with you, my peace I give unto you. . . . Let not your heart be troubled..." (John 14:27).
- A. Our world is desperately searching for peace. Education, psychology, atomic build-up—these have all failed to bring peace.
- B. Many Christians have been caught up in the hurry-scurry of our busy times and lack peace also.
- C. Christ provided His peace and gives it to those who receive it by faith. Daily acceptance of His peace brings real and lasting serenity (Phil. 4:6–7).

IV. Practice the Power of Christ
". . . all power is given unto me in heaven and in earth" (Matt. 28:18).
- A. Many Christians become exhausted and frustrated because they disregard God's help and try to live in their own strength.
- B. They fail to realize that finite power is insufficient for today's living. Christ's infinite power is needed.
- C. Paul declared that he could do all things through Christ (Phil. 4:13). The power of Christ is available to us through faith. Let us accept and practice it.

10

P-R-A-I-S-E the Lord

"Enter into his gates with thanksgiving, and into his courts with praise: be thankful unto him, and bless his name" (Ps. 100:4).

Christians should offer P-R-A-I-S-E:

I. P-urposefully
   A. Christ's life here on earth was set with purpose. He performed with a specific goal in mind—redemption for mankind.
   B. We must live with intent and purpose also, being deliberate in our praise to God, seeking to glorify Him, being a blessing to others (Ps. 150).

II. R-esponsively
   A. Many fail to respond to God's blessings. They forget, neglect, or worse yet, feel they have earned their possessions and do not need to thank God.
   B. Everything we are or own comes in response to His blessings. He deserves our praise. "Every good gift . . . is from above . . ." (James 1:17).

III. A-ffectionately
   A. Some Christians praise the Lord in a light, flippant manner. Their lives usually reveal a lack of spiritual depth.
   B. Let us praise the Lord with sincere and loving adoration. His great love and sacrifice make Him worthy of all our praise (Ps. 145:8–10).

IV. I-nspirationally
A. Christians who praise the Lord are an inspiration to others. Many are searching for joy and will go where it can be found.
B. Joyful praise is contagious. When a person is inspired to praise the Lord, others will join in, and soon many are praising the Lord together (Ps. 148:11–13).

V. S-pontaneously
A. Hidden sins or pride may prevent some from praising the Lord spontaneously.
B. Praises to God should flow naturally and without restraint. We can never praise Him sufficiently (Ps. 146:1–2).

VI. E-verlastingly
A. Christians should begin now to praise the Lord. In heaven the saints of all ages and the holy angels praise Him eternally.
B. Declare with the psalmist, "Every day will I bless thee; and I will praise thy name for ever and ever" (Ps. 145:2).

11

T-E-A-C-H Me, Lord

"Shew me thy ways, O LORD; teach me thy paths. Lead me in thy truth, and teach me..." (Ps. 25:4–5).

Just as children should begin learning from birth, so God's children should begin learning from Him following their new birth.

I. T-rust
"Trust in the Lord with all thine heart..." (Prov. 3:5).
   A. Many Christians suffer needless worry and frustration. They wait until their own resources are exhausted before they trust in the Lord.
   B. We must go to the Lord first and then continue trusting Him while doing our best to improve and remedy our situation. God's power never fails (Prov. 3:5).

II. E-ndurance
"Let us hold fast the profession of our faith without wavering" (Heb. 10:23).
   A. Some Christians are short on endurance. When oppression strikes, they resort to self-pity or fall into the "slough of despond."
   B. We must follow Christ's example of endurance. We must keep on keeping on by faith, assured that "He is faithful that promised" (Heb. 10:23).

III. A-ffection
"... for charity [love] shall cover the multitude of sins" (1 Peter 4:8).
   A. Many Christians are quick to criticize and find fault. A lack of love causes them to look for the bad, not the good in others.

B. Christ gave His life on the cross because He loved us. We must be kind, compassionate, and understanding, "having the same love, being of one accord, of one mind" (Phil. 2:2).

IV. C-ommitment
"Present your bodies a living sacrifice, holy, acceptable unto God..." (Rom. 12:1).
- A. Many Christians have not made a complete commitment to God. They hold in reserve certain portions of their lives for selfish purposes.
- B. If we are to please God, we must commit our all to Him—our wants, ways, work, wealth—everything. ". . . he is able to keep that which I have committed unto him . . ." (2 Tim. 1:12).

V. H-eaven Is Home
"Lay not up for yourselves treasures upon earth . . . But lay up for yourselves treasures in heaven . . ." (Matt. 6:19-20).
- A. Millions live as though they were going to take their possessions into eternity with them. How foolish! All must be left behind (1 Tim. 6:7).
- B. Heaven is the Christian's home. We must be faithful to do God's work and support His kingdom. A crown of righteousness awaits the faithful (Rev. 2:10).

12

The Good Shepherd and His Sheep

Scripture Reading: John 10:1–28

"I am the good shepherd: the good shepherd giveth his life for the sheep" (John 10:11).

The following points should serve to encourage our faith and trust in Christ, the Good Shepherd.

I. The Sheep Listen to Him
". . . and the sheep hear his voice: and he calleth his own sheep by name . . ." (John 10:3).
- A. Sheep are quick to hear and heed the shepherd's voice. His voice calms their fears and reassures them in times of danger.
- B. Christians must be alert to the voice of Christ, the Good Shepherd. His comfort brings healing and His commands give direction (John 10:27).

II. The Sheep Are Led by Him
". . . he goeth before them, and the sheep follow him. . ." (John 10:4).
- A. The shepherd goes ahead of his sheep and leads them in safe places. The sheep follow their shepherd with confidence.
- B. Christ, the Good Shepherd, goes before His sheep also. The path has been screened by His love. We can follow Him with safety and assurance (Ps. 23).

III. The Sheep Are Loyal to Him
"And a stranger will they not follow, but will flee from him . . ." (John 10:5).
- A. Many profess to follow Christ but they are unfaithful. Their thoughts, words, deeds, and actions betray them.
- B. We must be loyal to Christ, the Good Shepherd. We must reject wrong-doing and strive to do those things that are pleasing in His sight (1 John 3:22).

IV. The Sheep Live Through Him
"I am come that they might have life, and that they might have it more abundantly" (John 10:10).
- A. The human race was under the penalty of death, but Christ, the Good Shepherd, paid the debt for us (Rom. 6:23).
- B. If we listen to, are led by, and are loyal to Christ, the Good Shepherd, in this life, we shall live with Him eternally in the life to come (John 10:28).

13

Christian Duties in the World

". . . Fear God, and keep his commandments: for this is the whole duty of man. For God shall bring every work into judgment, with every secret thing, whether it be good, or whether it be evil" (Eccles. 12:13–14).

Christians have a duty to God, themselves, and others. To please God they should be:

I. Holy in a Sensuous World
"Sanctify yourselves therefore, and be ye holy: for I am the LORD your God" (Lev. 20:7).
  A. Lewdness and lust abound everywhere. Suggestiveness and sexual perversion are promoted in the movies, television, radio, and the printed page.
  B. Christians must keep their thoughts pure. They must be on guard concerning what they see, hear, say, do, and the places they frequent (Phil. 4:8).
  C. Christians must quickly replace evil thoughts with good. They must depend on the Holy Spirit to help them shun the wrong and do the right (1 Thess. 5:22–23).

II. Happy in a Saddened World
"Happy is he . . . whose hope is in the LORD his God" (Ps. 146:5).
  A. Christians are admonished to rejoice in the Lord always. Total commitment to God's will brings peace and joy (Phil. 4:4–7).
  B. Millions are trying to find happiness in alcohol, drugs, and sinful pleasure, but there is more sorrow and sadness than ever before.
  C. Christians must exemplify the Lord by being joyful. Happiness in Christians will show the world that Christ is the way to true joy (Prov. 16:20).

III. Helpful in a Suffering World
"Blessed is he that considereth the poor: the LORD will deliver him in the time of trouble" (Ps. 41:1).
- A. Starvation, disease, divorce, and child abuse abound. Millions are suffering on this earth.
- B. When Christ was here He spent much of His time helping the suffering. He healed the sick, comforted the sorrowing, and forgave the guilt-ridden.
- C. We must help those suffering in our day. We must feed hungry people, seek to ease the burdens of the oppressed, and enlighten those who are spiritually blind (1 John 3:17–18).

IV. Hopeful in a Sinful World
"Now the God of hope fill you with all joy and peace in believing, that ye may abound in hope, through the power of the Holy Ghost" (Rom. 15:13).
- A. Many Christians believe there is no hope for our sinful world. They declare that our society is doomed and nothing can be done to save it.
- B. Christ has not changed. His power has not diminished. He can still save to the uttermost (Heb. 7:25).
- C. We must be hopeful when it comes to the salvation of the lost. We must recognize that as long as there is life there is still hope. "In hope of eternal life, which God . . . promised before the world began" (Titus 1:2).

14

God Brings Deliverance

"He brought me up also out of an horrible pit, out of the miry clay, and set my feet upon a rock, and established my goings. And he hath put a new song in my mouth, even praise to our God: many shall see it, and fear, and shall trust in the LORD" (Ps. 40:2-3).

To be delivered means to be set free from restraint, to be released. God delivers us through:

I. Salvation
"He brought me up out of an horrible pit, out of the miry clay . . ." (Ps. 40:2).
- A. Our world is bound by the chains of sin, selfishness, greed, and graft.
- B. Many Christians are in bondage to troubles, worry, and affliction. God is our only hope. He has promised deliverance to those who call upon Him (Rom. 10:13). Healing and help await those who trust in the Lord (Ps. 91:14–15).
- C. God forgives and cleanses those who confess their sins and commit their will to His will. Salvation brings deliverance (1 John 1:7–9).

II. Stability
". . . and set my feet upon a rock, and established my goings" (Ps. 40:2).
- A. Today's world is seeking security in possessions, education, and by arming itself with destructive weapons, but there is less security than ever before.
- B. God is the refuge of Christians. He holds them steady when they are threatened by floods, tornadoes, atomic confrontation, and every destructive force.
- C. God brings stability to those who trust in Him. He delivers them and sends His angels to guard and protect them day by day (Ps. 91:10).

III. Singing

"And he hath put a new song in my mouth, even praise unto our God..." (Ps. 40:3).

A. Every good song carries a message of hope. God delivers from discouragement, disappointment, and despair when Christians express songs of praise to Him.

B. Singing the songs of Zion causes the soul to rise above the petty trifles of life. It lifts one from the humdrum of existence into the presence of the Almighty.

C. When Christians keep a song of praise on their lips and in their hearts, Satan is defeated, God is glorified, and they are delivered (Rom. 14:17).

IV. Service

"... many shall see it, and fear, and shall trust in the LORD" (Ps. 40:3).

A. Many Christians lack victory because they fail to serve God responsibly. They are too busy with selfish and personal pursuits.

B. Deliverance awaits Christians who lovingly help the less fortunate, comfort the aged and lonely, and give of their means to help share Christ with those on foreign soil who have never heard the gospel of Jesus Christ (1 Cor. 3:9).

C. Our Christian influence often extends farther and testifies to more than we know. When others see what Christ does for us, they will want Him, too (2 Cor. 5:17, 20).

15

God's W-O-R-D Teaches

"For whatsoever things were written aforetime were written for our learning, that we through patience and comfort of the scriptures might have hope" (Rom. 15:4).

God speaks through His own message to man. Christians can learn how to live for Him by reading, meditating, and using God's W-O-R-D. It teaches:

I. W-orship of God
"God is a Spirit: and they that worship him must worship him in spirit and in truth" (John 4:24).
   A. Many people pursue temporal gain instead of eternal riches. They worship silver and gold, diamonds and pearls, houses and land (Exod. 34:14).
   B. We should seek to lay up treasures in heaven. Earthly treasures pass away but heavenly treasures are everlasting (Matt. 6:19–21).
   C. We must worship God "in spirit and in truth." Prayer, meditating on God's Word, and faithfulness to the means of grace all assist in our "worship of God."

II. O-bedience to God
". . . Obey my voice, and I will be your God, and ye shall be my people . . ." (Jer. 7:23).
   A. Many believers know what they should do but fail to do it. They disobey God through neglect and lack of concern.
   B. We must heed the voice of God above the advice of friends or the dictates of our own desires. God must have first place in our lives.
   C. Christ was obedient to death on the cross, there to atone for our sins. We receive eternal salvation when we obey Him by meeting His requirements of repentance and faith (Heb. 5:8–9).

III. R-eliance on God

"Trust in the LORD with all thine heart; and lean not unto thine own understanding (Prov. 3:5).

A. Sometimes Christians fail to rely on God as they should. They depend on their own strength or the support of others instead of appropriating God's strength.
B. Our world is filled with frustration, destruction, and sinfulness. We need greater ability and understanding than we possess.
C. We must rely on God. Finite strength is weak and faltering, and we fail when we depend on our own poor powers. God's infinite power and wisdom never fail (Ps. 28:7).

IV. D-irection by God

". . . when he, the Spirit of truth, is come, he will guide you into all truth . . ." (John 16:13).

A. Many Christians lack direction in their daily living. Their lives are frustrated. They do not have the courage and strength to do God's work effectively.
B. Christians must totally commit their will to God's will. When they do, the Holy Spirit cleanses and fills them with His love and empowers them for service.
C. God-directed Christians are effective workers. They help the needy, comfort the lonely, and share Christ with the unsaved (Prov. 3:6).

16

How to Overcome Temptation

"The Lord knoweth how to deliver the godly out of temptations..." (2 Peter 2:9).

Many Christians do not know how to combat Satan's strategies when it comes to battling temptation. The following suggestions should help Christians to be overcomers.

I. Restrain Yourself
"But I keep under my body, and bring it into subjection..." (1 Cor. 9:27).
- A. To win over temptation you must first decide which way you are going to take—the right way or the wrong way. Indecision never works.
- B. When you have determined to shun the wrong and do the right, you must practice self-discipline. Set rules and limits for yourself and force yourself to obey them.
- C. You must stay away from Satan's territory. Tempting yourself by seeing how close you can get to sin without doing wrong must be avoided.
- D. Self-restraint is a necessity when it comes to winning the battle over temptation. The body must be brought "into subjection," as the apostle Paul said. "Blessed is the man that endureth temptation . . ." (James 1:12).

II. Resist the Devil
"... Resist the devil, and he will flee from you" (James 4:7).
- A. When Jesus was tempted of Satan, He resisted by denouncing him. "Then saith Jesus unto him, Get thee hence, Satan" (Matt. 4:10).
- B. You must do as Jesus did: Resist and denounce the devil. No matter how many times he returns, continue to resist Satan's suggestions (James 4:7).

C. You can resist the devil by becoming involved in the work of God. Get busy doing something positive for others—offer your moral or physical assistance to one in need, seek to uplift one who is in spiritual need, or speak a word of encouragement to one who is depressed.

D. The more you resist the devil, the easier it will become to withstand future attacks (1 Peter 5:9–10).

III. Rely on the Lord

". . . God . . . will not suffer you to be tempted above that ye are able; but will . . . also make a way to escape, that ye may be able to bear it" (1 Cor. 10:13).

A. The promises of God never fail. Just as Jesus used them to overcome temptation, you can do likewise (Ps. 119:11).

B. The prayers of the righteous prevail. You can win over temptation by asking God to help you and then believe Him to do so immediately (Matt. 26:41).

C. The power of God will help you overcome. Finite power is not enough; it often weakens and falters. But God's infinite power never fails.

D. You can overcome temptation by restraining yourself, resisting the devil, and above all, relying on the Lord (2 Peter 2:9).

17

Miracle of Healing

Scripture Reading: Luke 18:35–43

"And Jesus saith unto him, Receive thy sight: thy faith hath saved thee" (Luke 18:42).

The day of miracles is not past. Christ is still performing them today. The promise remains, "according to your faith be it unto you" (Matt. 9:29).

I. The Restriction
". . . a certain blind man sat by the way side begging: And hearing the multitude pass by, he asked what it meant" (Luke 18:35–36).
- A. This poor man was restricted because of his blindness. He was forced to beg for his livelihood.
- B. Millions lack the blessing that salvation brings because they are blinded by sin. Many Christians are restricted in their service for God because they are afflicted and need His healing touch.

II. The Recognition
"They told him, that Jesus . . . passeth by . . . And he cried, saying, Jesus . . . have mercy on me" (Luke 18:37–38).
- A. This afflicted man "looked to" Jesus in spite of his blindness.
- B. We must look to Jesus in spite of our sorrow, burdens, and affliction. His miracle of healing is sufficient for those who call on Him in faith (Matt. 9:21–22).

III. The Rebuke
"And they . . . rebuked him . . . but he cried so much the more . . . have mercy on me" (Luke 18:39).
- A. This poor blind man did not let the rebuke of the people stop him. He kept on calling on Jesus.
- B. We must not be concerned about what others might think, say, or do. The miracle of healing can happen if we keep on praying and believing.

IV. The Request

"And Jesus ... asked him ... What wilt thou that I shall do. ... And he said, Lord, that I may receive my sight" (Luke 18:40–41).

A. This man came to Jesus willingly and made his request specific—"Lord, that I may receive my sight."

B. We must come to Jesus, also (Matt. 11:28). And we must be specific with our requests. Vague, uncertain prayers never receive definite answers.

V. The Receiving

"And Jesus said ... Receive thy sight: thy faith hath saved thee. And ... he received his sight ..." (Luke 18:42–43).

A. The miracle of healing came to this man not only because of his determination but also because of his faith.

B. We can receive miracles today, providing we have faith. Everything is possible to those who believe (Mark 9:23).

VI. The Rejoicing

"And ... he ... followed him, glorifying God: and all the people ... gave praise unto God" (Luke 18:43).

A. This man was blind but now he could see. It is little wonder that he followed and glorified Jesus.

B. We must follow and glorify Jesus also. The more we recognize and praise Him for the miracles He performs in our lives, the more He will continue to send.

18

Slow Down and Live

Scripture Reading: John 11:1–44

"Jesus answered, Are there not twelve hours in the day?..." (John 11:9)

Jesus was not lazy or slothful. He was never late. Jesus never ran to get the job done. He was not caught up in the hurry, scurry of His day. We must try to live as Jesus did.

I. Physically
"For ye shall not go out with haste . . . for the LORD will go before you . . ." (Isa. 42:12).
- A. Our world is filled with people who are in a hurry. They rush to their jobs, then they rush home. They dash here, there, and everywhere.
- B. Millions do not take time to pray, read God's Word, or attend church faithfully. They fail to give God first place in their lives. They need to slow down and live.
- C. Jesus never ran to get the job done. He awaited God's time and direction. We must not be caught up in the hurry, scurry of the throngs but take (and make) time for God. Let us follow the example of Jesus (Ps. 27:14).

II. Mentally
"Let this mind be in you, which was also in Christ Jesus" (Phil. 2:5).
- A. The minds of many people are running in high gear. They are atuned to the noise and clamor of the day, wherein is more frustration than ever before.
- B. Some are afraid to be honest with God and themselves. They avoid confessing their sins, using constant activity to distract themselves from the real cause of their frustrations. Sins must be confessed and resolved.

C. Jesus had no hang-ups. He was honest, open, and able to face Himself, His heavenly Father, the world, and Satan. We must yield our will to God's will and totally commit our lives to Him. "The peace of God . . . shall keep your hearts and minds" (Phil. 4:7).

III. Spiritually

"Be still, and know that I am God . . ." (Ps. 46:10).

A. Millions are so preoccupied with personal pursuits that their spiritual life is disregarded. They are too busy making money, buying cars, owning houses, and caring for possessions.

B. It isn't wrong to have possessions—if we keep them in proper perspective. We must take time to help the needy, work for social justice, and seek out souls for Christ. God must have the preeminence in our life.

C. Jesus always put first things first. He admonished us to "seek ye first the kingdom of God, and his righteousness; and all these things shall be added unto you" (Matt. 6:33). Let us slow down and live—physically, mentally, and spiritually.

19

Spirit-Filled Christians

". . . and they were all filled with the Holy Ghost, and they spake the word of God with boldness" (Acts 4:31).

When Christians totally surrender their will to God's will, the Holy Spirit cleanses and fills their hearts with God's love. They are also empowered for service. Following are some of the things they are enabled to do.

I. Spirit-filled Christians Stand Up
"But Peter, standing up . . . lifted up his voice, and said unto them . . . hearken to my words" (Acts 2:14).
- A. Before Peter was filled with the Holy Spirit he denied Christ three times. He was ashamed to be known as a Christian, fearing ridicule and persecution.
- B. Many Christians today are afraid to stand up for the right. Like Peter they fail to witness for Christ as they should.
- C. The Holy Spirit imparts needed courage to totally committed Christians, enabling them, like Peter, to take their stand for Christ.

II. Spirit-filled Christians Settle Down
". . . through death, to present you holy . . . if ye continue in the faith grounded and settled . . ." (Col. 1:22-23).
- A. Many Christians are unstable, undependable, and unsettled. They are up one day and down the next. You never know where to find them.
- B. Christians should be rooted and grounded in the faith. They should be trustworthy, dependable in their home and family life, and faithful in doing God's work.
- C. The Holy Spirit establishes, strengthens, and settles those who are completely yielded and filled with God's love (1 Peter 5:10).

III. Spirit-filled Christians Are Sealed-in
". . . after that ye believed, ye were sealed with the Holy Spirit of promise" (Eph. 1:13).
  A. Christians who are sealed with the Holy Spirit are kept safe and secure in a dangerous and insecure world. They are *in* the world but not *of* the world.
  B. Spirit-filled Christians are guided by the Holy Spirit—to mountaintop delights and through the valley's depths evoked by frustrating difficulties (John 16:13).
  C. Sealed-in Christians enjoy the abiding presence of the Holy Spirit. God's power endues them for service, and Christ's peace brings comfort and assurance (Phil. 4:7).

IV. Spirit-filled Christians Are Sent Out
". . . after that the Holy Ghost is come . . . ye shall be witnesses unto me . . ." (Acts 1:8).
  A. Many default where God's work is concerned. Some neglect; some make excuses; some simply turn a deaf ear to God's call.
  B. Spirit-filled Christians delight in doing God's work. The Holy Spirit empowers them to lift the ailing, encourage the discouraged, and witness to the lost (John 14:12).
  C. When God sends Christians out, He goes with them. He speaks through them—the right words, to the right people, at the right time, in the right place (Matt. 10:20).

20

The Apple of God's Eye

Scripture Reading: Psalm 17

"Keep me as the apple of the eye, hide me under the shadow of thy wings" (Ps. 17:8).

God's people are very special to Him. He watches over and cares for them in this life and will be with them in the life to come. We are the apple of God's eye.

I. He Hears Us When We Cry
". . . O Lord, attend unto my cry, give ear unto my prayer . . ." (Ps. 17:1).
  A. Many people cry on the shoulder of a friend, or perhaps of a counselor. While the help they receive may be good, it is likely to be temporary and limited.
  B. We must cry unto the Lord when we are distressed or disappointed. He is lasting, unlimited, and understanding. He truly cares.
  C. We should appreciate the listening ear of another, but realize that finite power often falters and fails. God's infinite power never fails. He always hears us when we cry. We are the apple of God's eye.

II. He Helps Us When We Try
"Hold up my goings in thy paths, that my footsteps slip not" (Ps. 17:5)
  A. God did not promise to take us to heaven on flowery beds of ease. He did not promise to do everything for us, but He did promise to help us.
  B. When we do our best, and that is not good enough, God will do the rest. Our strength (however small it may be), plus God's help, can handle any situation (Phil. 4:13).
  C. We must trust in the Lord with all our heart and He will give us direction (Prov. 3:5). He will help us when we try, for we are the apple of His eye.

III. He Hides Us When We're Shy
". . . hide me under the shadow of thy wings" (Ps. 17:8).
- A. The apostles came to Jesus weak and worn from doing God's work. Jesus said, ". . . come ye yourselves apart into a desert place, and rest awhile . . ." (Mark 6:31).
- B. Christians become exhausted physically, mentally, and spiritually. At times they feel like the psalmist: "Oh that I had the wings of a dove! for then would I fly away, and be at rest!" (Ps. 55:6).
- C. We must trust and rest in the Lord when we feel shy, inadequate, and unable to go on. He will renew, revive, and replenish our resources. We are the apple of God's eye.

IV. He Holds Us When We Die
". . . I will behold thy face . . . I shall be satisfied, when I awake, with thy likeness" (Ps. 17:15).
- A. Some Christians avoid talking or thinking of death. They believe death will be a time of aloneness.
- B. Christians need not fear crossing the "valley of the shadow of death," for Jesus promised, ". . . I will never leave thee, nor forsake thee" (Heb. 13:5). "Precious in the sight of the LORD is the death of his saints" (Ps. 116:15).
- C. And the Lord will be with us in the hereafter, too. We shall be "safe in the arms of Jesus"—always. ". . . them also which sleep in Jesus will God bring with him" (1 Thess. 4:14). We shall always be the apple of God's eye.

21

The Dimensions of Love

"That Christ may dwell in your hearts by faith; that ye, being rooted and grounded in love, may be able to comprehend with all saints what is the breadth, and length, and depth, and height" (Eph. 3:17-18).

God's love is so immense it cannot be adequately described. This message only skims the surface. At best we fall short when it comes to exploring the dimensions of His great love.

I. Love Spans the Widest Ocean
"May be able to comprehend . . . what is the breadth . . ." (Eph. 3:18).
- A. Some Christians' love is narrow in scope. It includes only their own family, and perhaps a few friends. They fail to be the blessing they should be.
- B. Christ's love is broad in its expanse. It spans the widest ocean and includes the whole world. Christ's love is not limited by color, creed, or condition (John 3:16).
- C. Our love must extend to others. We must love the unlovable, assist the needy, comfort the lonely, and share Christ with the lost.

II. Love Travels the Longest Road
"May be able to comprehend . . . what is the . . . length . . ." (Eph. 3:18).
- A. Some people's love is short-lived; it is here today and gone tomorrow. Their love changes with their whims and the rise and fall of their emotions.
- B. Christ's love is eternal. It traveled the longest road—to Calvary. In every trouble, sorrow, disappointment, or misunderstanding, Christ loves you.
- C. Our love must keep on keeping on, too, despite the difficulty. There is no defense against a love that doesn't give up (1 John 3:16).

III. Love Descends the Deepest Valley
"May be able to comprehend . . . what is the . . . depth . . ." (Eph. 3:18).
- A. Most human love fails to reach the deepest valley, the darkest night, the depths that human sin, suffering, and sorrow have reached.
- B. Christ's love reaches deeper than the stain of sin has gone. It reaches down to the dregs of the sorrowing, suffering, guilt-ridden millions of the world.
- C. We must share Christ's love with compassion and sympathy. We must not "love in word (only) . . . but in deed and in truth" (1 John 3:18).

IV. Love Climbs the Highest Mountain
"May be able to comprehend . . . what is the . . . height" (Eph. 3:18).
- A. The love of many Christians is stymied by their own selfish desires and ambitions. They forfeit countless blessings.
- B. Christ's love climbed the highest mountain—Mount Calvary—for us. No matter how steep and difficult our climb, Christ is there to lift and love (Gal. 2:20).
- C. Like Christ we must expand the dimensions of our love. Love spans the widest ocean, travels the longest road, descends the deepest valley, and climbs the highest mountain.

22

The Essentials of Life

". . . I am come that they might have life, and that they might have it more abundantly" (John 10:10).

Jesus Christ is the essence of life. He supplies the necessities for this life and also for the life that is to come. Christ is:

I. The Bread of Life

". . . I am the bread of life; he that cometh to me shall never hunger" (John 6:35).

A. Bread is known as the staff of life. It represents food for the starving millions of the world. Bread is necessary to life.

B. Christ is declared to be the Bread of Life. He satisfies the innate hunger of the soul. He keeps those who partake of the life He gives from spiritual starvation (John 6:33).

C. We accept Christ through repentance and faith. He removes our guilt and assures us of eternal life. He satisfies our spiritual hunger (John 6:51).

II. The Water of Life

"And whosoever will, let him take the water of life freely" (Rev. 22:17).

A. Water is essential to life. Our bodies are largely composed of water. Without it we would soon die.

B. Christ is the Water of Life. Water is also a type of the Holy Spirit. He quenches our spiritual thirst and empowers us for service.

C. When we totally surrender our will to God, He cleanses and fills us with His love. His love then reaches out through us (John 7:37–39).

III. The Light of Life
"... I am the light of the world: he that followeth me shall not walk in darkness ..." (John 8:12).
A. Light is necessary to life. Without light our world would return to its original chaotic condition—"... without form, and void; and darkness ..." (Gen. 1:2).
B. Untold millions are in spiritual darkness—stumbling, falling; and without direction. People need the Light of Life to guide them.
C. Christ is the Light of the World. By following Him we find direction, protection, fellowship, and cleansing (1 John 1:5–7).

IV. The Love of Life
"In this was manifested the love of God ... God sent his only begotten Son ... that we might live through him" (1 John 4:9).
A. Love is essential for living. Everyone needs to love and to be loved.
B. Christ loved so much, He died in our stead. Neither angels, kings, nor presidents could atone for our sins. Christ alone could and did (Gal. 2:20).
C. Not only must we love God, but we must love others, too. We can reach a helping hand around the world with our monetary support and prayers. Love leads to eternal life (1 John 3:14).

23

The Greatest Love

"For God so loved the world, that he gave his only begotten Son, that whosoever believeth in him should not perish, but have everlasting life" (John 3:16).

This text explains the greatest love—God's love. Human love falls short. When we accept Christ as Savior and Lord, we receive "the greatest love."

I. The Person
"For God so loved the world..." (John 3:16).
   A. "... God created the heaven and the earth" (Gen. 1:1). God made the firmament, the sun, moon, and stars. He created the fish in the sea, the fowl in the air, and the beasts in the forest.
   B. "God created man in his own image..." (Gen. 1:27). God created man for fellowship, but man sinned when he disobeyed and thereby lost fellowship with God.
   C. The wages of sin is death. However, God loved humankind so much He provided a way to restore them to fellowship. God's love is the greatest.

II. The Price
"... that he gave his only begotten Son..." (John 3:16).
   A. God paid the supreme price for the restoration of human fellowship.
   B. Kings, presidents, and angels could not atone for the sins of humankind. God gave "His only begotten Son" to die in our stead.
   C. We can never repay God but we can glorify Him. We can extend His love to others. We can share Christ with the unsaved (1 John 3:16).

III. The People
"... *that whosoever believeth in him should not perish* ..." *(John 3:16).*

A. Forgiveness and cleansing await the rich and poor, the black and white, great and small alike. No one is excluded.
B. Those with financial, social, or political standing get no preference. Those with physical and mental infirmities are not overlooked by God.
C. Salvation is for all who repent of their sins and believe on Jesus Christ. The greatest love—God's love—extends to all (1 John 5:1–5).

IV. The Prospect
"... *but have everlasting life*" *(John 3:16).*

A. Many people seek selfish gain and sinful pleasures. Their reward is fleeting and will soon pass away forever.
B. The Christians' prospect is "everlasting life." Jesus has gone to prepare a place for those who love Him. He will return to receive them unto Himself (John 14:1–3).
C. We must be constrained by "the greatest love"—God's love. We can lend a helping hand to the needy, speak an encouraging word to the lonely, and witness to the lost about the Person, the price, the people, and the prospect.

24

The Holy Spirit in Believers

"Even the Spirit of truth; whom the world cannot receive, because it seeth him not, neither knoweth him: but ye know him; for he dwelleth with you, and shall be in you" (John 14:17).

The Holy Spirit lives within totally committed Christians. He brings purity, peace, purpose, and power to their lives.

I. The In-heritance
". . . that they may receive forgiveness of sins, and inheritance among them which are sanctified by faith that is in me" (Acts 26:18).
- A. Inheritance: The new birth makes Christians eligible for the fullness of the Spirit.
- B. Christians must set themselves apart to God (1 Peter 3:15). We must surrender our will in total yieldedness to God's will (Rom. 6:13).
- C. The Holy Spirit sanctifies totally committed Christians (Rom. 15:16). He cleanses, fills, and keeps their "whole spirit and soul and body" (1 Thess. 5:23).

II. The In-dwelling
". . . he shall give you another Comforter, that he may abide with you for ever" (John 14:16).
- A. The Holy Spirit is the Christian's indwelling Comforter. He has promised never to leave nor forsake His own (Heb. 13:5).
- B. Our world has desperately sought security and serenity through grasping possessions, pleasure, and power, but has failed.
- C. The Holy Spirit is the Christian's source of security and serenity. His abiding presence gives comfort and assurance even in a desperately troubled world.

III. The In-struction
". . . the Holy Ghost . . . shall teach you all things, and bring all things to your remembrance . . ." (John 14:26).
- A. Millions depend on themselves and others for direction. Their lives are filled with frustration and confusion.
- B. Spirit-filled Christians can know where they are and where they are going. They depend on the Holy Spirit for guidance.
- C. The Holy Spirit works, speaks, and loves through totally committed Christians. They delight in obeying His instructions (John 16:13).

IV. The In-volvement
"Ye shall receive power, after that the Holy Ghost is come upon you: and ye shall be witnesses unto me . . ." (Acts 1:8).
- A. Many Christians fail to get involved in God's work. Some are too busy. Some are too shy. Some are spiritually lazy.
- B. Spirit-filled Christians are endued with power for service. They are enabled to help lead the lost to Christ and to reach out to others unselfishly.
- C. The inheritance, indwelling, instruction, and involvement of the Holy Spirit in the lives of Christians enable them to lay up treasures in heaven, their eternal reward (Matt. 6:20).

25

The Jesus W-A-Y

"Jesus saith unto him, I am the way..." (John 14:6).

Some take the way of least resistance. Some take their own stubborn way. The best way to take is the Jesus W-A-Y. It is the:

I. W-inning Way
"But thanks be to God, which giveth us the victory through our Lord Jesus Christ" (1 Cor. 15:57).
- A. Persons who frequently fail in their sundry attempts in life use such terms as "bad luck" and "jinxed," making excuses for their lack of success. Actually, their pessimistic attitude and lack of faith are to blame.
- B. Jesus was always a winner. He overcame temptation, trial, testing, and even death. He defeated Satan with a positive faith and implicit trust in His heavenly Father.
- C. The "Jesus way" is the winning way. All Christians should win over Satan, sin, and self. With His help they can.
- D. However, victory and success are promised only to those who, like Christ, practice optimistic faith and implicit trust (Ps. 37:3–5).

II. A-chieving Way
"I can do all things through Christ which strengtheneth me" (Phil. 4:13).
- A. Many Christians fall short when it comes to working for God, but they work long hours for personal gain.
- B. Jesus kept busy doing His Father's work. He healed the sick, gave sight to the blind, raised the dead, and saved the lost. His achievements held eternal value.

C. We must take, or make, time for the things which are of lasting value. We should share in the work of the church, support it with our finances, visit the sick, comfort the bereaved, provide for the helpless, and share Christ with the lost.
D. As we give Christ first place in our lives, the Holy Spirit will enable us to lay up eternal rewards (Mark 9:41).

III. Y-ielded Way
". . . yield yourselves unto God, as those that are alive from the dead . . ." (Rom. 6:13).

A. Many want to win and achieve but they stop short. The "Jesus way" also includes living the yielded way. When Christians depend on their own strength, or lean on doctors, loved ones, friends, or others, they fail.
B. Help received from others should be appreciated, but we must put our trust in God's infinite power. Finite power is uncertain and fallible, but God's omnipotent power never fails.
C. Jesus prayed, ". . . not my will, but thine, be done" (Luke 22:42). His will was yielded to the Father's will. We must give our hopes, plans, and desires to God in total surrender (Prov. 3:5-6).
D. The "Jesus way" is the best way not only in this life, but in the world to come. It leads to eternal happiness.

26

The Value of Faith

"Above all, taking the shield of faith, wherewith ye shall be able to quench all the fiery darts of the wicked" (Eph. 6:16).

The importance of faith cannot be overly emphasized. Faith is necessary to salvation, serenity, and security. We please God and receive His gifts when we believe.

I. Faith Brings Pardon
". . . believe on the Lord . . . and thou shalt be saved . . ." (Acts 16:31).
- A. When God sent an earthquake to deliver Paul and Silas from the Philippian jail, the keeper asked in desperation, "Sirs, what must I do to be saved?" (Acts 16:30).
- B. Many people are trying to get to heaven on their good works, but this is impossible to do. Regardless of one's intensity and sincerity, self-effort cannot bring pardon.
- C. The requirements for forgiveness of sins are the same today as they were in Paul's day. Those who repent must simply believe on the Lord Jesus Christ (Eph. 2:8–9).

II. Faith Brings Purity
". . . purifying their hearts by faith" (Acts 15:9).
- A. Many Christians fail to totally surrender to God. They reserve certain portions of their lives for themselves. They lack faith in God.
- B. God will settle for nothing less than a complete yieldedness of our wills to His will. We must trust and obey, giving Him first place in our lives.
- C. The Holy Spirit purifies Christians who unreservedly yield self-will to God's will. They are sanctified by faith (Acts 26:18).

III. Faith Brings Peace
"Thou wilt keep him in perfect peace, whose mind is stayed on thee: because he trusteth in thee" (Isa. 26:3).
- A. Our world is desperately searching for peace. We try to attain it by stockpiling nuclear weapons, by using psychology, by gaining possessions, and by indulging in pleasure, but we fail.
- B. There is no real and lasting peace outside of God, and we receive Him only through faith. Peace cannot be earned or purchased. It is God's free gift to His children.
- C. Simple trusting faith brings peace. By committing our lives to do the will of God and letting Him bear the responsibility, we receive God's peace. It keeps our hearts and minds (Phil. 4:7).

IV. Faith Brings Power
". . . all things are possible to him that believeth" (Mark 9:23).
- A. Nations must remain strong if they are to exist in this competitive age. Political and military power is necessary for survival.
- B. The power of God is the greatest need of man. His hope and help are found in the gospel of Jesus Christ, the power of God unto salvation (Rom. 1:16).
- C. Faith brings God's power. Sins are forgiven, burdens are lifted, problems are solved, and disappointments are turned into His appointments when we believe (Matt. 9:29).

27

What's Your Problem?

"Many are the afflictions of the righteous: but the LORD delivereth him out of them all" (Ps. 34:19).

All people have troubles, and most are trying desperately to find solutions for their problems. Christ is the answer. He is able to solve all our problems, but He needs our cooperation.

I. Confession Brings Salvation
"If we confess our sins, he is faithful and just to forgive us our sins, and to cleanse us from all unrighteousness" (1 John 1:9).
  A. Every individual needs forgiveness, "for all have sinned, and come short of the glory of God" (Rom. 3:23). Repentance and faith bring forgiveness.
  B. The Holy Spirit cleanses and fills Christians with God's love when they surrender their wills to His will.
  C. Salvation solves problems of guilt, resentment, and the bondage of sin. It also prepares Christians for the next life.

II. Commitment Brings Serenity
". . . he is able to keep that which I have committed unto him . . ." (2 Tim. 1:12). "Thou wilt keep him in perfect peace, whose mind is stayed on thee" (Isa. 26:3).
  A. Greed and violence abound today. Nations and individuals are destroying one another in an attempt to find peace.
  B. Power, pleasure, and possessions do not bring peace of mind and soul.
  C. Real, lasting peace comes from God. When we commit our way to God, trust Him implicitly, ". . . he shall bring it to pass (Ps. 37:5).

III. Confidence Brings Security
"This is the confidence that we have in him . . . whatsoever we ask, we know that we have the petitions that we desired of him" (1 John 5:14-15).
   A. Millions of people are troubled. They are searching for security in many ways—establishing savings accounts, making investments, and acquiring property.
   B. Earth's treasures do not bring joy and security. Savings are eaten up by inflation. Possessions wear out, rust, and deteriorate. They are temporal.
   C. Faith in God solves security problems. God is eternal and all-powerful. He never fails those who place their confidence in Him (Phil. 4:19).

IV. Christlikeness Gives Service
"Herein is our love made perfect . . . because as he is, so are we in this world" (1 John 4:17).
   A. Christ spent His life on earth giving service to mankind. He healed the sick, fed the hungry, clothed the naked, and forgave the sinful.
   B. We, too, must assist the poor and needy, comfort the sick and lonely, and share Christ's love with the unsaved.
   C. Doing God's work with Christlikeness brings hope to ourselves, healing to others, and honor to God (James 2).

28

The Dynamics of L-O-V-E

"In this was manifested the love of God toward us, because that God sent his only begotten Son into the world, that we might live through him" (1 John 4:9).

The letters L-O-V-E represent four words that may help us to better understand the victory, virtues, and value of God's love.

I. L-iberates
"If the Son therefore shall make you free, ye shall be free indeed" (John 8:36).
  A. Millions around the world are living in sin's bondage. They are bound by social, sensual, and secular entrapments.
  B. Christ's love brings physical, mental, and spiritual freedom to all those who accept Him. When we repent, surrender to God's will, and believe, we are set free (John 8:32).
  C. Liberation brings joy. Joy is attractive to others and will move them to accept Christ's love.

II. O-vercomes
". . . be of good cheer; I have overcome the world" (John 16:33).
  A. When we totally commit our lives to Christ, the Holy Spirit fills us with God's love. We increase our love by praying for and befriending others.
  B. Love wins over hatred, strife, jealousy, and resentments. There is no defense against love. "Charity never faileth" (1 Cor. 13:8).
  C. Christ's love enabled Him to overcome ridicule, persecution, and death on the cross. His love and presence in our lives helps us to overcome (1 John 4:4).

III. V-olunteers

"Have fervent charity (love) . . . for charity (love) shall cover the multitude of sins" (1 Peter 4:8).

A. Love exerts deliberate and resolute action. Love goes the second mile, returns good for evil, gives and forgives, looks for the good, and overlooks the bad (Eph. 4:32).

B. Christ volunteered, of His own free will, to pay the penalty for our sins. He was not forced to go to the cross but He died willingly, compelled by His great love.

C. God's dynamic love causes us to volunteer to help the needy and neglected, comfort the lonely, and share Christ's love with the unsaved (Eph. 6:7–8).

IV. E-ndures

"Heaven and earth shall pass away, but my words shall not pass away" (Matt. 24:35).

A. Ours is a materialistic society. Millions are selling their souls for things that wear out, rust, and decay.

B. Love is eternal, for "God is love" and He is from everlasting to everlasting. Christ insisted that we lay up treasures in heaven, not on earth (Matt. 6:19–21).

C. We must give God first place in our lives and seek to do those things that are pleasing in His sight. We must take time to pray, praise, and practice God's love. His love is dynamic. It works energetically today and it will endure in the life to come.

29

Are You for Real?

"And ye shall seek me, and find me, when ye shall search for me with all your heart" (Jer. 29:13).

Many people ask, "Is God for real—His salvation, help, miracles?" The question should be "Are you for real?" If so:

I. You Will Find Pardon
"Godly sorrow worketh repentance to salvation . . ." (2 Cor. 7:10).
- A. Millions of people need forgiveness. They are loaded down with the guilt of sin. It destroys them physically, mentally, and spiritually.
- B. When you come to Christ "for real," repenting with godly sorrow for all your sins, He will forgive you and remove your guilt. You will find pardon (Isa. 55:7).

II. You Will Find Purity
"And God, which knoweth the hearts, bare them witness, giving them the Holy Ghost . . . purifying their hearts by faith" (Acts 15:8-9).
- A. Many Christians fail to totally yield their lives to Christ. They want to hold on to certain portions for selfish interests. They are not "for real."
- B. If you want purity of heart, you must be "for real," surrendering your will, ways, and wants to Christ without reserve. The Holy Spirit will cleanse and make you spiritually whole (Heb. 9:14).

III. You Will Find Peace
"And the peace of God . . . shall keep your hearts and minds through Christ Jesus" (Phil. 4:7).
- A. Our world is searching for peace through negotiations, nuclear expansion, and nuclear freeze, but there is still little hope for peace. Even many Christians lack peace.

B. To have Christ's peace, you must be "for real." You must love God and others, trust, obey, and believe. ". . . my peace I give unto you. . . . Let not your heart be troubled . . ." (John 14:27).

IV. You Will Find Power
"Who are kept by the power of God through faith . . ." (1 Peter 1:5).
A. We live in a power-hungry world. Nations seek power to dominate or destroy other nations. People want power to inflate sagging egos. Christians need power to live victoriously.
B. Are your motives right? Do you have faith? Christ will empower you for service if you are "for real" (Phil. 4:13).

V. You Will Find Purpose
"According to the eternal purpose which he purposed in Christ Jesus our Lord" (Eph. 3:11).
A. Many people fail because they lack purpose. They are not "for real," but they are seeking for self-gratification instead of God's approval.
B. Have faith, hope, and love. Seek God's will for your life. Give Him first place and you will find purpose for living (Eph. 1:9).

30

Attaining to Spiritual Heights

"Because he hath set his love upon me . . . I (will) deliver him: I will set him on high, because he hath known my name" (Ps. 91:14).

There is no standing still in the Christian life. We are either going forward or losing ground. The following points should help us gain spiritual heights.

I. Entrust Yourself to the Lord
"Trust in the LORD with all thine heart; and lean not unto thine own understanding" (Prov. 3:5).
  A. Many Christians fail to attain spiritual heights because they depend on their own strength and understanding.
  B. Finite power flounders and fails but God's infinite power never fails.
  C. We make gain spiritually when we surrender totally to God's will, giving Him first place in our lives (Matt. 6:33).

II. Endure the Sufferings of the Lord
". . . Christ also suffered for us, leaving us an example, that we should follow his steps" (1 Peter 2:21).
  A. Christ suffered rejection, persecution, and death. Because He suffered, we may come in simple faith and receive forgiveness and cleansing.
  B. We must endure testings and trials.
  C. Christians who suffer most are often the greatest blessing to others. We are ill-equipped to help those who are troubled if we have had no trouble ourselves (2 Cor. 1:4).

III. Enjoy the Salvation of the Lord
"Rejoice in the Lord alway: and again I say, Rejoice" (Phil. 4:4).
- A. Many unhappy Christians wear sad faces and set a poor example for others to follow.
- B. Christians should be the happiest people on earth because they are redeemed, cleansed, and on their way to heaven.
- C. Unhappy Christians should pray as the psalmist did, "Restore unto me the joy of thy salvation . . ." (Ps. 51:12).

IV. Engage in the Service of the Lord
". . . I have chosen you, and ordained you, that ye should go and bring forth fruit . . ." (John 15:16).
- A. Many Christians fail to make spiritual growth because they are too busily engaged in their own pursuits. They have not totally committed their time, talent, and treasure to God.
- B. Trusting, enduring, happy Christians love to do God's work. They assist the less fortunate, comfort the lonely, share Christ with the unsaved, and bear much fruit (John 15:5).

31

Coping with the "Daily Grind"

"Blessed be the Lord, who daily loadeth us with benefits, even the God of our salvation" (Ps. 68:19).

Christians are seldom tempted to commit atrocious criminal acts. It is the small, almost insignificant everyday happenings that usually take them to the point of defeat.

I. Recall God's Comforting Promises
"Whereby are given unto us exceeding great and precious promises . . ." (2 Peter 1:4).
- A. Because many Christians neglect God's promises, they are ill-equipped to face the "daily grind."
- B. There is power, healing, and help in God's Word. We search for the promises that fit the special area of our needs and rest upon them.
- C. God's promises are the Christian's weapon. They enable us to cope. Let us read them, meditate on them, write them down, remember them, use them (Heb. 4:12).

II. Receive God's Calming Peace
"And the peace of God . . . shall keep your hearts and minds through Christ Jesus" (Phil. 4:7).
- A. The "daily grind" becomes upsetting and frustrating to many Christians. They forget God's admonition to "Fret not thyself because of evil doers . . ." (Ps. 37:1).
- B. Jesus said, ". . . my peace I give unto you. . . . Let not your heart be troubled . . ." (John 14:27).
- C. When we allow God's calming peace to envelope us—body, mind, and soul—He enables us to handle the "daily grind."

III. Reclaim God's Controlling Power
"Strengthened with all might, according to his glorious power . . ." (Col. 1:11).
- A. Many Christians try to cope with frustrating circumstances in their own strength and therefore fail.
- B. Finite power is insufficient. We must depend on God's infinite power. He is still in control and never fails.
- C. Each day we should proclaim with Paul, "I can do all things through Christ which strengtheneth me" (Phil. 4:13).

IV. Recognize God's Continuing Presence
". . . and, lo, I am with you alway, even unto the end of the world" (Matt. 28:20).
- A. Sometimes Christians may feel lonely while their fellow workers are engaged in pursuing sinful interests.
- B. Christians should remember that they are never alone, for God is always with them.
- C. Their fellowship is with the Lord. His promises, peace, power, and presence give assurance and enable them to cope with the "daily grind" (Isa. 41:10).

32

Effective Workers for Christ

"We then, as workers together with him, beseech you also that ye receive not the grace of God in vain" (2 Cor. 6:1).

Effective workers are the great need of the church world. The following points tell us how Christians can become effective workers for Christ.

I. Get Counsel from Christ
". . . the Spirit of truth . . . will guide you into all truth . . ." (John 16:13).
  A. Christians should be sensitive to the Holy Spirit's leadings when sharing Christ with the unsaved. He will give guidance and direction.
  B. Christian workers who fail to get counsel from Christ sometimes "go in where angels fear to tread," doing more harm than good.
  C. When we depend on the Holy Spirit, He will lead us to the right place, at the right time, and help us say the right thing to the right person (John 14:26).

II. Give Compassion Like Christ
"Jesus . . . was moved with compassion . . . because they were as sheep not having a shepherd . . ." (Mark 6:34).
  A. Jesus had compassion on the heavy laden, the lonely, the less fortunate, and the lost (Matt. 11:28).
  B. Christian workers must feel compassion. They should empathize with others, putting themselves in their place.
  C. Everyone is weak and needy in certain areas. As we give love and compassion, others will be blessed (1 Peter 3:8).

III. Gain Confidence Through Christ
"I can do all things through Christ which strengtheneth me" (Phil. 4:13).
  A. Many Christians want to be effective workers for Christ but are hindered by a lack of confidence.
  B. Christian workers need to gain God-confidence rather than self-confidence.
  C. Through prayer, God's Word, and faith, we recognize the greatness of God. His power, purpose, and presence will enable us to become effective workers (1 John 5:14–19).

IV. Go Courageously for Christ
"Go ye therefore, and teach all nations . . . and, lo, I am with you alway . . ." (Matt. 28:19–20).
  A. Christ gave Himself for us. We must give of our time, talent, and treasure for Him.
  B. We must be faithful in our church attendance and financial support. We should be ready to share Christ with the unsaved as opportunity affords.
  C. If we go courageously for Christ in this life, He will go with us through death and be with us in the life to come (Isa. 41:10).

33

Get with It for Christ

"Wherefore he saith, Awake thou that sleepest, and arise from the dead, and Christ will give thee light" (Eph. 5:14).

Every child of God needs to get with it for Christ. The following points should encourage sinners to become Christians and Christians to become better Christians.

I. Get Up—Come to Christ
"Come unto me, all ye that labour and are heavy laden, and I will give you rest" (Matt. 11:28).
 A. Millions need to get up and come to Christ. Sinners are dead in trespasses and sins (Eph. 2:1).
 B. Get up from your doubts, fears, and resentments and come to Christ. Get up from selfish pursuits, the love of money and pleasure, and come to Christ.
 C. ". . . and him that cometh to me I will in no wise cast out" (John 6:37).

II. Get Down—Confess to Christ
"If we confess our sins, he is faithful and just to forgive us our sins, and to cleanse us from all unrighteousness" (1 John 1:9).
 A. Millions need to confess their sins to Christ with humility and true repentance. He is ready to forgive (Eph. 1:7).
 B. Christians should confess their faults, failures, and frustrations, repenting of their lethargy and lack of concern for the things of God.
 C. "Humble yourselves in the sight of the Lord, and he shall lift you up" (James 4:10).

III. Get In—Commit to Christ
". . . present your bodies a living sacrifice, holy, acceptable unto God . . ." (Rom. 12:1).
- A. Many try to hold onto Christ and the world simultaneously. This is impossible to do. We cannot serve two masters (Matt. 6:24).
- B. We must surrender all to Christ, stop playing around the edges, and ". . . launch out into the deep . . ." (Luke 5:4).
- C. Christians should get involved for Christ.

IV. Get Out—Conquer for Christ
"Go ye . . . teach all nations . . . and, lo, I am with you alway, even unto the end of the world" (Matt. 28:19–20).
- A. Many Christians are not with it when it comes to doing God's work. Some are too busy with personal pursuits, some are shy, some are spiritually lazy.
- B. Get with it for Christ. Get out and fight the evil, pray for world leadership, and share Christ with the unsaved.
- C. Go for Christ and He will go with you (Matt. 28:20). Forget self-interests, self-consciousness, and self-ease. Get out. Conquer for Christ.

34

H-A-P-P-Y Christians Are . . .

"Whoso trusteth in the LORD, happy is he" (Prov. 16:20).

There are both happy and unhappy Christians. In today's troubled world, God wants His people to be H-A-P-P-Y.

I. H-opeful Christians
"Happy is he . . . whose hope is in the LORD his God" (Ps. 146:5).
- A. Sometimes Christians lose hope and become unhappy. Discouraging situations cause them to become despondent and depressed.
- B. Happy Christians are hopeful Christians. They need never lose hope, for God is present to help in time of need, regardless of circumstances (Rom. 12:12).

II. A-chieving Christians
"For thou shalt eat the labour of thine hands: happy shalt thou be . . ." (Ps. 128:2).
- A. Some Christians are unproductive when it comes to doing God's work. They sit with folded hands and find fault with those who are getting the job done.
- B. Happy Christians are busy Christians. They pursue their assignments with joy. "Be not overcome of evil, but overcome evil with good" (Rom. 12:21).

III. P-rayerful Christians
"Be careful for nothing; but in every thing by prayer . . . with thanksgiving . . ." (Phil. 4:6).
- A. Many Christians are slack when it comes to prayer. They attempt too much in their own strength and fail.

B. Christians should not worry and fret. They should pray instead, taking their daily duties, as well as their problems to God. He is able to help them (Phil. 4:7).

IV. P-raising Christians
"Sing praises to God, sing praises: sing praises unto our King, sing praises" (Ps. 47:6).
  A. Millions of Christians are overwhelmed with personal, job, church, national, and world problems. They fail to praise the Lord. As a result, they are unhappy.
  B. Happy Christians form a habit of praising the Lord. The more they praise the Lord, the more blessings He sends—and the greater blessing they become to others (Ps. 113:3).

V. Y-ielding Christians
"If ye know these things, happy are ye if ye do them" (John 13:17).
  A. The failure to completely yield their will to God is perhaps the greatest cause for lack of harmony and unhappiness among Christians.
  B. Regardless of situations and circumstances, totally yielded Christians can and should be happy. God takes the responsibility for their lives. His grace and strength are sufficient (2 Cor. 12:9).

35

How to H-E-A-R the Word

". . . He that heareth my word, and believeth on him that sent me, hath everlasting life . . ." (John 5:24).

Scripture admonishes us to "hear the word of the Lord." The following points should help us understand what it means to truly H-E-A-R God's Word.

I. H-eed the Word
"Thy word is a lamp unto my feet, and a light unto my path" (Ps. 119:105).
  A. "To heed" means "to pay close attention to: take careful notice of" (Webster). Millions today ignore and disregard God's Word.
  B. Hearing God's Word brings condemnation to the sinful. When exposed to the light of God's Word, they feel guilty for their sins.
  C. When sinners heed the Word and repent of their sins, they find forgiveness. When Christians heed the Word and make a total commitment to God, they are cleansed and made spiritually whole (Heb. 2:1).

II. E-mbrace the Word
"Great peace have they which love thy law . . ." (Ps. 119:165).
  A. Many Christians do not embrace God's Word. They suffer conflict and loss because of their neglect.
  B. The Bible holds the answers to earth's problems. We need to hide it in our hearts as a protection against sin (Ps. 119:11).
  C. Christians must embrace God's Word, hold it close, love and cherish it. We should declare with the psalmist, "O how love I thy law! It is my meditiation all the day" (Ps. 119:97).

III. A-ccept the Word
"So then faith cometh by hearing, and hearing by the word of God" (Rom. 10:17).
- A. Many Christians live beneath their privilege. They heed and embrace God's Word, perhaps, but fail to take it to themselves and apply it to their personal needs.
- B. We must know the Bible well and memorize its promises, but we must also accept it by faith as God's personal message to us.
- C. Believe that God is speaking directly to you through His Word. His promises are for you personally. They never fail (2 Peter 1:4).

IV. R-ejoice in the Word
"I rejoice at thy word, as one that findeth great spoil" (Ps. 119:162).
- A. The psalmist rejoiced in the Word as if he had found an invaluable treasure. God's Word is great, rich, and rewarding.
- B. God's Word points the way to pardon, purity, peace, and power. It offers satisfaction, sustenance, stability, and security.
- C. Those who rejoice in the Word of God now shall also rejoice eternally (Matt. 24:35).

36

How to Use God's Word Effectively

"For the word of God is quick, and powerful, and sharper than any two-edged sword..." (Heb. 4:12).

Many Christians do not know how to make full use of God's Word. The following points should assist us in using the Word of God more effectively.

I. Hear the Word
"... faith cometh by hearing, and hearing by the word of God" (Rom. 10:17).
- A. We are admonished throughout the Scriptures to "hear the word of the Lord." Hearing God's Word is the first step toward using it effectively.
- B. Through the hearing of the Word of God we are made aware of the availability of salvation.
- C. "... He that heareth my word, and believeth on him that sent me, hath everlasting life ..." (John 5:24).

II. Heed the Word
"We ought to give the more earnest heed to the things which we have heard..." (Heb. 2:1).
- A. Millions fail to heed God's Word as they should. Some take it lightly, others ignore it.
- B. We must "give the more earnest heed," pay close attention, to the Word of God.
- C. We find direction for our life when we heed the Word. "Thy word is a lamp unto my feet, and a light unto my path" (Ps. 119:105).

III. Hide the Word
"Thy word have I hid in mine heart..." (Ps. 119:11).
- A. Many Christians fail to meditate on God's Word. They are not equipped to handle times of special stress and need.
- B. We must hide God's Word in our heart. Not only should we read and meditate on the promises, we should memorize them, too.
- C. When times of desperation come and trouble threatens to overwhelm us, God's Word gives security and peace (Ps. 119:165).

IV. Hold Forth the Word
"Holding forth the word of life..." (Phil. 2:16).
- A. A lighthouse sends forth its beams to help ships escape the dangers of a tempestuous sea and direct them safely into harbor.
- B. We must hold forth the Word of God and help those lost on the raging sea of life to find their way home.
- C. God's Word leads the weary traveler to the haven of safety, rest, and eternal life (2 Peter 1:4).

37

How to Win Over Depression

"We are troubled on every side, yet not distressed; we are perplexed, but not in despair" (2 Cor. 4:8).

Everyone has troubles, trials, and testings, but those who seek God's help need not sink into despondency.

I. Stop Looking Downward—Start Looking Upward
   "Why art thou cast down, O my soul? . . . hope thou in God: for I shall yet praise him . . ." (Ps. 42:5).
   A. Discouragement is one of the greatest hindrances to the Christian life. Too often Christians dwell on the dark and dreary rather than the bright and sunny side of life.
   B. The more we look downward, the more depressed we become, and the more depressed we become, the more we look downward.
   C. Start looking upward now and say with the psalmist, "I will lift up mine eyes. . . . My help cometh from the LORD . . ." (Ps. 121:1–2).
   D. Little children are light-hearted and carefree. They trust their parents implicitly for their needs. Our heavenly Father wants His children to live with simple, trusting faith.

II. Stop Looking Inward—Start Looking Outward
   ". . . [Christ] died for all, that they which live should not henceforth live unto themselves, but unto him . . ." (2 Cor. 5:15).
   A. Christians who become self-centered are miserable and depressed. They feel unimportant, unwanted, and unloved.
   B. Start looking outward. God loves you. Ask Him to forgive, cleanse, and fill you with His love and compassion (Phil. 4:7).

C. Lose yourself in service for God and others. Assist the needy. Comfort the sick and lonely. Share Christ with the unsaved (Matt. 10:38–39).

D. Recognize your God-given talents and develop them. Start looking outward. Be rewarded in this life and win eternal rewards in the world to come.

III. Stop Looking Backward—Start Looking Forward

". . . forgetting those things which are behind, and reaching forth unto those things which are before" (Phil. 3:13).

A. Many Christians become depressed because they look almost exclusively to past accomplishments. They lack vision for the future and fail to advance God's kingdom on earth.

B. Start looking forward even when results are slow coming in. If you are faithful, God will send the increase in His own time and way (1 Cor. 3:6–7).

C. Start looking forward. You can do something for God and others. A smile, a touch, a kind word, a prayer—little can be much when God is in it.

D. Look forward with anticipation and hope. The best is yet to come. There will be no sorrow, suffering, or separation in our heavenly home (Rev. 21:4).

38

Jesus Christ, the Rock

". . . they drank of that spiritual Rock that followed them: and that Rock was Christ" (1 Cor. 10:4).

The following points should encourage Christians to be diligent for Christ. He is:

I. The Rock of Salvation
". . . exalted be the God of the rock of my salvation" (2 Sam. 22:47).
   A. Because of his disobedience to God, man was doomed to death. "For the wages of sin is death; but the gift of God is eternal life through Jesus Christ our Lord" (Rom. 6:23).
   B. Jesus Christ becomes the Rock of our salvation when we repent of our sins and believe Christ for forgiveness. Total commitment brings cleansing and the abiding presence of the Holy Spirit.
   C. Christ is our defense against the penalty of sin. He is the Rock of Salvation (Ps. 62:2).

II. The Rock of Stability
"He . . . set my feet upon a rock, and established my goings" (Ps. 40:2).
   A. Sin creates instability. Jesus Christ, the Rock of Salvation, is also the Rock of Stability. He wants us to be steadfast, established in the faith (1 Peter 5:10).
   B. When we are surrounded with confusion and perplexity, Christ will hold us steady in an unsteady world.
   C. With our trust in Christ, we can say with the psalmist, ". . . when my heart is overwhelmed: lead me to the rock that is higher than I" (Ps. 61:2).

III. The Rock of Shelter
"... *as the shadow of a great rock in a weary land" (Isa. 32:2).*
- A. When the storms of life are raging, Christ is the Rock of Shelter in whom we can safely hide.
- B. Through the stress and exhaustion of our busy times, Christ gives rest and healing. He restores our strength (Ps. 37:7).
- C. Those who trust in the Lord can declare, ". . . the rock of my strength, and my refuge, is in God" (Ps. 62:7).

IV. The Rock of Splendor
". . . let the inhabitants of the rock sing, let them shout from the top of the mountains" (Isa. 42:11).
- A. Christians should exalt the Lord more. They should praise Him continually and work for Him faithfully.
- B. Christians should be the happiest people on earth. They are freed from guilt and condemnation and are promised a home in heaven.
- C. Christ is the Rock of Salvation, the Rock of Stability, the Rock of Shelter, and the Rock of Splendor. He shall continue to be the Rock of Splendor when we see Him face to face. There we shall praise Him eternally (Rev. 5:12–13).

39

Reasons to be Cheerful

"A merry heart maketh a cheerful countenance: but by sorrow of the heart the spirit is broken" (Prov. 15:13).

Are there any reasons to be cheerful in this chaotic, devastated world? The following points show us why Christians can be cheerful:

I. Power of Christ to Forgive Sins
". . . be of good cheer; thy sins be forgiven thee . . . the Son of man hath power on earth to forgive sins . . ." (Matt. 9:2, 6).
   A. The power of Christ to forgive sins offers the greatest possible reason for rejoicing.
   B. Silver and gold cannot buy forgiveness of sins. Medicine and science cannot produce forgiveness. Heavenly angels do not have the power of forgiveness.
   C. Jesus Christ can reach down in the gutter of despair and lift the penitent soul from the miry clay of sin and set him free from the bondage of sin (Matt. 9:6).

II. Provision of Christ to Overcome
"In the world ye shall have tribulation: but be of good cheer; I have overcome the world" (John 16:33).
   A. Who can overcome in a world filled with troubles such as we live in?
   B. Jesus conveyed the message that we can overcome the world: "Be of good cheer; I have overcome the world."
   C. In a world torn by war, strife, and chaos, we can be at peace. "That in me ye might have peace"—a truly, great reason to be cheerful (John 16:33).

III. Protection of Christ When in Danger
"Be of good cheer, Paul: for as thou hast testified of me in Jerusalem, so must thou bear witness also at Rome" (Acts 23:11).
   A. Christians who witness for Christ may be subjected to persecution and threat.
   B. Witnessing for Christ endangered Paul's life. ". . . the chief captain, fearing lest Paul should have been pulled in pieces of them . . ." (Acts 23:10).
   C. Christ will protect us as He did Paul until we have completed His work. He is still saying, "Be of good cheer . . ." (Acts 23:11).

IV. Presence of Christ to Banish Fear
". . . Jesus spake unto them, saying, Be of good cheer; it is I; be not afraid" (Matt. 14:27).
   A. When the disciples were tossed and driven on the stormy sea, Christ's presence calmed their fears.
   B. The presence of Christ will calm the winds and waves and heal the hurts in our lives when the storms come.
   C. We must practice Christ's presence with us, for He is still saying, "Be of good cheer; it is I; be not afraid" (Matt. 14:27).

40

R-E-S-T in the Lord

"Rest in the LORD, and wait patiently for him" (Ps. 37:7).

Ours is a restless world. Millions are suffering turmoil and strife. Many Christians live beneath their privilege. Let us look at some means for securing R-E-S-T.

I. R-elax
"Be careful for nothing; but in every thing by prayer . . . and the peace of God . . . shall keep your hearts and minds . . ." (Phil. 4:6-7).
   A. Many Christians fail to relax as they should. Some fret about situations they are powerless to change.
   B. Some are overly ambitious, constantly pushing themselves beyond what they are able to accomplish.
   C. We must accept the inevitable, believing God is helping us in our daily assignments. When we relax from worry and fretting, we are able to "rest in the Lord" (Ps. 37:1, 8).

II. E-njoy
"Rejoice in the Lord alway: and again I say, Rejoice" (Phil. 4:4).
   A. Some Christians have lost the joy of salvation. They wear gloomy faces and spend their time complaining instead of praising the Lord for His blessings.
   B. Gloomy Christians should pray with the psalmist, "Restore unto me the joy of thy salvation" (Ps. 51:12).
   C. Rejoicing in the Lord enables us to rest in Him also, for we cannot truly enjoy ourselves unless we enjoy the Lord (Ps. 37:4).

III. S-erve

How much more shall the blood of Christ, who through the eternal Spirit offered himself without spot to God, purge your conscience from dead works to serve the living God?" (Heb. 9:14).

   A. Many Christians fail in God's service department. Their lives are cluttered, involved, and overwhelmed by their own affairs.
   B. We must make time for God, giving Him the preeminence (Col. 1:18).
   C. God helps us as we take time to work and witness for Him. We can rest in the Lord now and be assured of an eternal rest to come (Ps. 37:27).

IV. T-rust

"Commit thy way unto the LORD; trust also in Him" (Ps. 37:5).

   A. The best way to "rest in the Lord" is to "trust in the Lord." Trust means to lean on, rely on, and be confident.
   B. Too many Christians are leaning on their own strength and relying on material gain and selfish pursuits.
   C. When we surrender our will unreservedly to God's will, trusting in Him, we can "rest in the Lord" and "he shall bring it to pass" (Ps. 37:5).

41

The Christian's Stand

Scripture Reading: Eph. 6:11–18

Wherefore take unto you the whole armour of God, that ye may be able to withstand in the evil day, and having done all, to stand. Stand therefore..." (Eph. 6:13–14).

The Bible reveals much about the Christian's stand. God's Word deals with the why, where, when, and what of the Christian's stand. Christians should:

I. Stand Up
"For whosoever shall be ashamed of me and of my words, of him shall the Son of man be ashamed..." (Luke 9:26).
 A. Some Christians are afraid to stand up for the Lord. They may be shy, self-conscious, or simply lacking in spiritual stamina.
 B. When we stand up courageously for the Lord, He will be there to strengthen, steady, and sustain us.
 C. As good soldiers of Jesus Christ, we must stand up for Him (2 Tim. 2:3).

II. Stand Still
"... fear ye not, stand still, and see the salvation of the LORD..." (Exod. 14:13).
 A. When in difficulty, many Christians take quick and drastic actions which may bring devastating results.
 B. We need to stand still and wait for God's orders, as did Moses and the children of Israel before crossing the Red Sea.
 C. Stand still—wait in patience and faith for God's time to "go forward" (Exod. 14:15).

III. Stand By
". . . to be ready to every good work" (Titus 3:1).
A. To "stand by" means to be ready to do God's service, to be dependable and trustworthy. Many Christians are too busy with their own interests and pursuits.
B. We must yield our wills to God and be ready to say, be, do, and go where He wants.
C. We must be totally committed to God, giving Him first place in every facet of our lives (Matt. 6:33).

IV. Stand Fast
"For now we live, if ye stand fast in the Lord" (1 Thess. 3:8).
A. Many Christians are wishy-washy. You never know where to find them.
B. When there are mountains to climb, valleys to descend, and rivers to cross, we must "stand fast" in the Lord.
C. We must never give up. A crown of life awaits those who "stand fast" in the Lord (Rev. 2:10).

42

Today's Instant Society

Wait on the LORD: be of good courage, and he shall strengthen thine heart: wait, I say, on the LORD" (Ps. 27:14).

Today's society is traveling in high gear and at breakneck speed. People want everything now—and have failed to take time for God. They will pay the consequences. Today's society desires:

I. Instant Pleasure
". . . lovers of pleasures more than lovers of God" (2 Tim. 3:4).
- A. Today's society is seeking instant pleasure. Sex before marriage is common. Entertainment is replacing church attendance. Desecration of the Lord's Day is the norm.
- B. The Christian's pleasure should be morally uplifting and wholesome, but God's judgment will be upon those who disregard His commands (James 5:5).
- C. Christians should be faithful in prayer, Bible reading, and church attendance.

II. Instant Possessions
". . . a man's life consisteth not in the abundance of the things which he possesseth" (Luke 12:15).
- A. The desire for possessions has captured the hearts of millions in today's instant society. They want to get rich quick.
- B. Many will lie, cheat, steal, or kill to get rich. First Timothy 6:10 warns that "the love of money is the root of all evil."
- C. God must have first place in our lives (Matt. 6:33). We should lay up treasure in heaven, not on earth (Matt. 6:19–21).

III. Instant Popularity
"How can ye believe, which receive honour one of another . . ." *(John 5:44).*
- A. Millions want to be popular. Many risk their lives to attain fame.
- B. In school, office, or factory, it is easy to go along with the crowd. Many abuse drugs and resort to sexual promiscuousness, hoping to gain instant popularity.
- C. God's approval is most important. He will supply grace and courage if we seek the honor that comes from Him, not from men (John 5:44).

IV. Instant Promotion
"Pride goeth before destruction, and an haughty spirit before a fall" *(Prov. 16:18).*
- A. Sinful pride causes many to seek promotion without earning or deserving it. Often those attaining instant promotion are demoted just as quickly.
- B. We must be patient and humble in our quest for success. We should prepare adequately and work diligently (James 4:10).
- C. Promotion comes from God. He is the judge (Ps. 75:6–7). Some day we shall be instantly and eternally promoted to the land of peace, joy, and love.

43

You Don't Have to F-A-I-L

Lift up your eyes on high, and behold who hath created these things . . . for that he is strong in power; not one faileth" (Isa. 40:26).

If you are a Christian, you should not think of yourself as a failure. Despite bad luck, disappointing circumstances, or frustrating situations, you need not F-A-I-L if you heed the following points.

I. F-aith
". . . this is the victory that overcometh the world, even our faith" (1 John 5:4).
- A. Most Christians need to exercise more faith. It makes the difference between success and failure.
- B. Faith brings conversion, cleansing, confidence, and courage. Faith pleases God (Heb. 11:6).
- C. Our faith increases when we pray, read God's promises, practice biblical principles, and persevere (1 John 5:14–15).

II. A-ction
"But be ye doers of the word, and not hearers only . . ." (James 1:22).
- A. Some fail because they are afraid to take action, lest they do the wrong thing. Others are stubborn and set in their ways.
- B. Lazy people seldom succeed in any endeavor. Accomplishment calls for action. Faith without works is dead (James 2:14–18).
- C. We must act in faith through prayer. Confidence in God assures success. He helps us get the job done.

III. I-nsight
"If any of you lack wisdom, let him ask of God . . . and it shall be given him" (James 1:5).
- A. Insight is needed for success. Finite understanding is insufficient. We must have wisdom from above—God's infinite wisdom.
- B. Christians who totally commit their lives to God are promised guidance and direction from the Holy Spirit (John 16:13).
- C. We receive wisdom by asking God in unwavering faith (James 1:6–7).

IV. L-ove
"Charity [love] never faileth" (1 Cor. 13:8).
- A. Marriages fail, homes are shattered, churches are closed because of a lack of love, not a lack of money. "Love never faileth."
- B. Love never fails because God never fails. "God is love." Loving God and others brings success in this life and eternal life in the world to come (1 John 4:7–9).
- C. Friends and loved ones may forsake us, wealth and possessions may pass away, youth and beauty may fade, but God's love will never fail. It is the greatest (1 Cor. 13:13).

44

Why We Should Keep F-A-I-T-H

"I have fought a good fight, I have finished my course, I have kept the faith" (2 Tim. 4:7).

It is most important that Christians maintain their confidence. The following are some good reasons why we should keep F-A-I-T-H.

I. F-aith Is Fortifying
". . . and this is the victory that overcometh the world, even our faith" (1 John 5:4).
- A. Forts were built during pioneer days for protection against danger. Faith fortifies us against the attacks of Satan.
- B. When Satan attacks through temptation, trial, discouragement, or affliction, faith will overpower the enemy. It brings victory (Eph. 6:16).

II. A-nswers Are Assured
"And all things, whatsoever ye shall ask in prayer, believing, ye shall receive" (Matt. 21:22).
- A. God answered prayer for Daniel in the lion's den, for the three Hebrew children in the fiery furnace, and for Paul and Silas in the Philippian jail. He is the same today.
- B. No matter how difficult the task, how desperate the circumstance, or how destructive the opposing forces, faith brings answers to prayer (Mark 9:23).

III. I-nfluence Is Important
"And he did not many mighty works there because of their unbelief" (Matt. 13:58).
- A. Jesus was unable to help those of His own country. His power was limited because of their unbelief, and His influence suffered.

B. We must keep faith. Our influence is important. Friends and loved ones need our prayers and encouragement. They are depending on us (James 5:15–16).

IV. T-imes Are Turbulent

"Why are ye so fearful? . . . ye have no faith?" (Mark 4:40).

A. As angry waves dashed their ship, the disciples grew frightened, but Jesus rebuked the wind. ". . . And the wind ceased, and there was a great calm" (Mark 4:39).
B. Today Christians may be dashed with turbulent winds of violence, hate, self-seeking. Jesus is still saying, ". . . Be not afraid, only believe" (Mark 5:36).

V. H-eaven's Our Home

". . . I have kept the faith: Henceforth there is laid up for me a crown of righteousness . . ." (2 Tim. 4:7–8).

A. Life on earth is saturated with trouble and trials. We often long for heaven. "For here have we no continuing city, but we seek one to come" (Heb. 13:14).
B. In heaven there will be no more sin, sorrow, suffering, or separation. We must keep faith for heaven is our home.